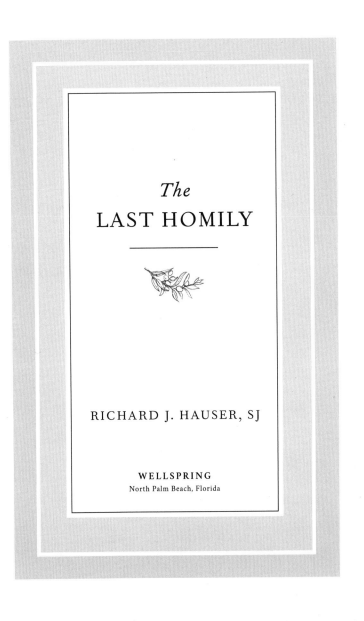

# *The*
# LAST HOMILY

RICHARD J. HAUSER, SJ

**WELLSPRING**
North Palm Beach, Florida

Published by Wellspring
All rights reserved.

Text of chapter two has been taken from transcript of the last homily
Fr. Hauser gave to the RENEW spiritual group in March 2018
(https://vimeo.com/260115218).

"Fr. Hauser's Vocation Story" is taken from a YouTube video
(https://www.youtube.com/watch?v=0NzdlkzP5Gk).

All photos copyright © Fr. Donald Doll, SJ. Used with permission.

Design by Madeline Harris

ISBN: 978-1-63582-065-2 (hardcover)

Library of Congress Control Number: 2018953473

10   9   8   7   6   5   4   3   2   1

Printed in the United States of America

*"Dick's great gift is to remind us to always look to our God, to speak to the one who loves us so deeply, and to find the Spirit of God in our hearts."*

—Fr. Don Doll, SJ

# *Contents*

# Introduction

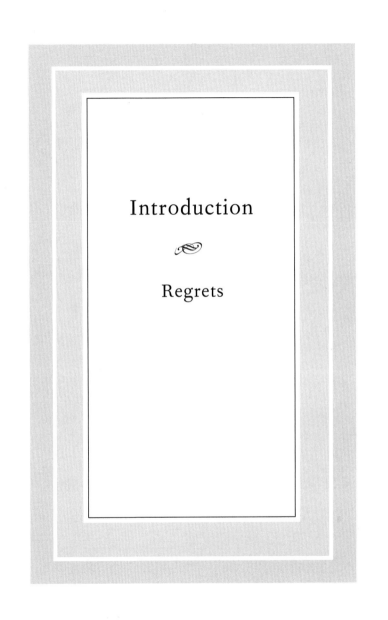

## Regrets

I have regrets. There are a lot of people who say they don't have any regrets, or they don't believe in having regrets. But I have regrets. One of my regrets is that I didn't make the time to get in the car or jump on a plane and visit Richard Hauser.

We had many wonderful email exchanges and a couple of joy-filled phone calls, but I never met the man.

I first became aware of him through his book *In His Spirit*. When I read it, I instantly knew I was

reading the best book I had ever read about the Holy Spirit. I remember putting it down and thinking two things: why haven't I heard of this book and this man, and I want to publish a new edition of this book through my own publishing company and share it with as many people as possible.

Each year when he saw how many copies we had sold, he would call me so excited that more than thirty years after it had first been published, we had found a new and larger audience for this fabulous book.

That book changed my life. It transformed my relationship with the Holy Spirit. Ten years before I read it, I wrote: "I never met anyone who relied too much on the Holy Spirit." It seems most people have an anemic relationship with the Holy Spirit. Ten years after I read Hauser's book, I still believe we don't call upon the Holy Spirit

anywhere near as much as we should in our day-to-day dealings with life and each other.

I have always believed that knowing you are going to die is in many ways a great blessing and a rare grace. It gives you a chance to prepare for the onward journey and to say good-bye to loved ones.

When people are told they are dying, they handle it in different ways, and how they handle it tells us something about who they are, what they value, and how they lived their lives.

We live in a culture that doesn't want to think about death. The result is that too many people go around unconsciously approaching life as if they are going to live forever. This false immortality usually leads people to live life in a way that is far from the virtues and values that bring the best out of us and others.

It seems we live in a time where people don't know how to live and they don't know how to die. We do both so poorly it seems. Knowing how to live is a beautiful thing. Knowing how to die is a rare grace. Fr. Richard Hauser possessed both of these blessings. I am sure he worked hard for both, and now, in this short volume he shares with us the secret to living well and dying well.

—Matthew Kelly

# One

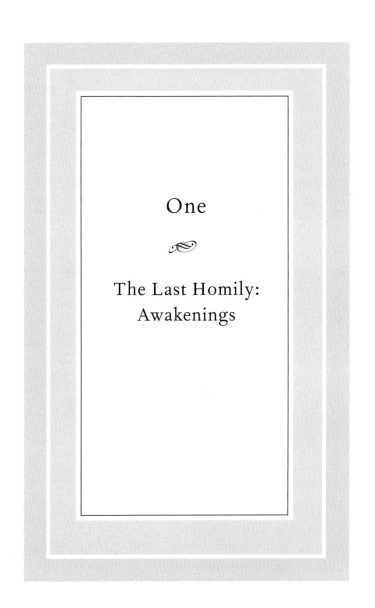

# The Last Homily:
# Awakenings

*On March 11, 2018, after having entered hospice, Fr. Richard Hauser preached his final homily to dear friends with whom he had shared the spiritual journey for forty years. He honestly shared what dying means to him in terms of learning more about what he believes and what he has yet to believe.*

Years ago, in a Jesuit recreation room, engaging in light conversation over drinks, my fellow priests and I had a discussion about what we would like on our tombstones. And rather spontaneously I replied, "He helped us recognize God's presence in our lives." And the realization hit me: that theme has run through all my teaching and all my writing.

I remember when it all started.

When I finished my graduate studies and came to Creighton University, I was asked to teach a beginning course in theology. What could I contribute to help students better understand their faith, and perhaps even cherish it? Christians affirm that through faith and baptism we receive a new life from God called sanctifying grace. Most Christians, however, have never identified this life in their experiences. Nor have college students. I decided to teach a course centered on helping students recognize this life. I called my course Faith and Experience. Most theology courses at Creighton dealt only with doctrine. I wanted to teach doctrine to the degree that it helped my students recognize their experience of God. The course was well received—in fact, it was very highly praised. And every subsequent course I taught contained as a main element the experience of God. Not simply doctrine, but how a particular doctrine pointed to the experience.

This was the post-Vatican II era. After calling for an ecumenical council, St. John XXIII prayed that the breath of the Spirit might rejuvenate the Church. And the pope's prayers were answered. The documents of Vatican II brought to our attention the role of the Holy Spirit, the sanctifier. Our experience of God is directly related to the actions of the Holy Spirit in our hearts, but so often we do not recognize that it is the Holy Spirit acting within us. My courses became eye-openers for students as they recognized for the first time that God was alive and well in their lives. And I subsequently

recognized that I myself had not really had an experience of the Holy Spirit before I started teaching courses at Creighton University.

My courses eventually evolved into articles I wrote for various journals and then into my three books. All three of my books focus on recognizing God's Spirit in our hearts. The first book, *In His Spirit*, has to do with recognizing God's Spirit and power in prayer. The second, *Moving in the Spirit*, has to do with recognizing God's Spirit and power in ordinary daily life. And the third book, *Finding God in Troubled Times*, has to do with recognizing God's Spirit and power in suffering. Through my own teaching and my own writing, I have discovered and appropriated the presence and action of God in my life at a level I never dreamed existed. In this way my work has been almost sacramental in uncovering the presence of

God, a presence that was there all the time, but which I had not recognized.

> This awakening of the self to the Spirit within our experience is a watershed in following Christ, a very important moment in our journey toward union with him. With this awakening, everything changes. Jesus moves from an acquaintance to a personal friend. This affects our daily living. Only after we have experienced this awakening can we speak of the goal of Christian spirituality as responding to the Spirit. Fidelity in responding to the Spirit will bring us into deeper and deeper union with Jesus and lead us to the highest union with God.[1]

Jesus said, "[I have come] that everyone who

---

[1] Excerpted from Fr. Hauser's book *In His Spirit*, available from DynamicCatholic.com.

believes in me may have eternal life" (John 3:15). Yet I have to confess: up to this point I've done almost no thinking about eternal life. The things I teach and preach and write about are all about finding God in daily life. The total focus of my spirituality has been learning to recognize God's presence in our ordinary daily lives. And I've taken for granted that if we do that, the continuity between this life and the next life will be respected. I still think that's the right focus: living this life with love for one another and not worrying about the afterlife. But that focus hasn't made me look forward to the next life.

I like this life, and I don't want to die. But now I think that my spirituality would be enhanced by a realization that this life is a prelude to the next life, and it would be good for me to think about that more often than I do. You see,

I think our culture weighs very heavy on us. It's very secular. Our culture teaches us that our happiness in this life is pretty much proportionate to our relationships, success, prosperity, and so forth. And our culture says zilch about the next life. I think most of us—including me—buy into that message. We kind of pretend that the next life will never occur.

Well, it's going to occur for me very soon.

Jesus said, "I'm going to prepare a place for you . . . that where I am you may be also" (John 14:2, 3). I may be blessed by the invitation to enter that next mode of life much sooner than I ever expected or wanted. So now I'm kind of desperately trying to switch my thinking to focus on that place, that promise.

Now, I'm not there yet, which I consider a big blessing. But as I reflect on passages like

"God so loved the world that he gave his only Son, that everyone who believes in him . . . might have eternal life" (John 3:16), I begin to see that our lives are preparations for that moment of transition.

The culture is not our friend. Our culture does nothing to help us prepare. I've been affected by our culture too, but I've also chosen to put my focus totally on loving and serving God in this life—which is what Jesus teaches. By doing so, though, I think I've somehow bracketed the possibility of death and a future eternal life. I think we all do. We think about going on vacation— taking a cruise or visiting Hawaii or something like that. For most of us, that's as good as it gets. But it's not as good as it gets. This has been a sobering consideration for me, but it's really a joyful consideration too.

My friend Kate has had to think about this with her husband, John. John died within the year after being diagnosed with cancer. Or my friend Mary—she had absolute joy as she lay in that hospice room. Her husband, Mike, would cry, and she'd say, "Oh, sober up! You're going to die pretty soon too, you know." She did much more to be ready for this than I have. Her faith had kicked in at some very deep level. It gave her the confidence that this was the next right step, and she was ready. She's been a model for me. I've been kind of praying to her now.

Don't you think our culture does us a disservice by not really even inviting us to think of a life beyond this one? Every ad you see on TV—I'm watching a lot of TV now—is all about health. Longevity. Overcoming cancer. As though the goal of life is to live physically as long as possible.

We are all products and victims of a culture which vaunts materialistic satisfaction as the chief means to happiness, continually reinforcing our internal tendencies toward selfishness.

Growth in union with the Lord demands the total effort of our being. We have the challenge of arranging patterns in our life in such a way that we live in habitual contact with the Spirit and allow the Spirit to guide all our activities. The effort is difficult because of many pressures moving us away from the Spirit toward self-centered actions and attitudes. Rather than respond to the Spirit, we often find ourselves responding to these pressures. The combination of our internal drive toward selfishness and the external pressures reinforcing this drive can motivate our life in a direction that is diametrically opposed to the message of the Gospel and the movement of the Spirit.

The solution is to build rhythms in our daily life that enable us to live habitually in tune with the Spirit and so become like Jesus in knowing and doing the Father's will in love. Practically this means that we must ask ourselves how God is calling us to love and serve him and his people, and this question must be asked on two levels. First, what is the state in life God wants for me, and second, how is he calling me on a day-to-day basis to fulfill this calling?[2]

My cancer is aggressive and fast-growing, and it has metastasized, but I was offered a special treatment. If the doctors can identify the cancer, in

---

[2] Excerpted from *In His Spirit* and *Moving in the Spirit*, both available from DynamicCatholic.com.

some cases they have drugs that deal directly with that particular cancer—not chemotherapy, which wipes out everything. But they don't tell you how the treatment might affect you. Terry, our nurse, looked up the side effects of the drugs my doctor was suggesting, and they were pretty devastating. They were worse than what I'm going through now. Plus, it's very expensive. If I don't know what quality of life I'm going to have, or what side effects I'll experience, do I want to gamble that maybe my life will be prolonged a little longer? Or do I simply want to embrace what seems to be God's call to me at this point in my life? It seems to me that God is calling me home and I ought to embrace that. So I don't feel badly about refusing treatment. I feel right about it.

So what occurs to you when you think about the next life? We've recently been preceded by three members of our group. It seems that God is calling us to awaken to the full Gospel message.

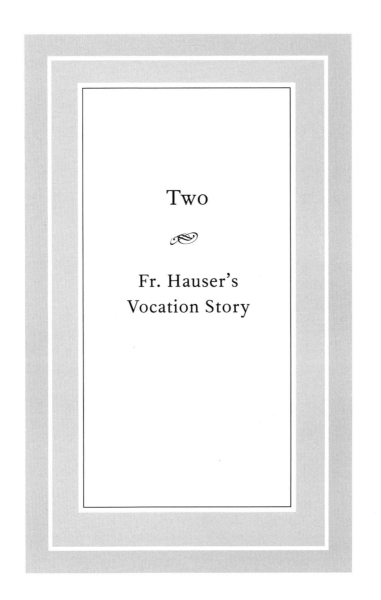

# Two

Fr. Hauser's
Vocation Story

Why I decided to become a Jesuit is an interesting story.

In January of my senior year of high school, we had a retreat at Marquette High, and the retreat master asked each of us if we wanted to become Jesuits. I said, "Absolutely not. I do not want to become a Jesuit; I do not now, nor have I ever wanted to become a Jesuit."

You see, my dad had given me a car for my senior year, I had a girlfriend that I had dated all through my junior and senior year, and I had

been accepted to Marquette University, where I planned to get both a law degree and a business degree. Becoming a priest was not in my plans.

But by March of my senior year, I was applying to the Jesuits. What happened?

Since my dad had given me a car, I began dropping in to our parish church after school. I'd sit in front of the image of the Sacred Heart and ask Jesus what I should do with my life. And whenever I thought about becoming a Jesuit, I had this overwhelming sense of joy and peace. I couldn't understand it, because I was still pretty much in a relationship with this girl, I enjoyed having my car, and I had dreams of being a successful upper-middle-class businessman and lawyer. What happened was that God pointed me to the Society of Jesus by giving me the experience of deep peace. When I was quiet in

God's presence, I had a type of joy I had never experienced before.

The only times I'd ever visited church before were on Sundays to fulfill the required religious obligation, but during this time I went during the week, and this is where God gave me the sign that he was calling me. That sign was a peace and joy and the sense that this was more right for me than anything else I could do, so I knew I had to try it.

The way I look at finding your vocation is by listening to your heart and not your head. Your head will tell you everything that society has conditioned you to think, but God touches your heart. When you listen to your heart, you'll hear God's voice. As the Bible says, "Today, when you hear his voice, do not harden your hearts" (Hebrews 3:15). When you follow your heart, you follow God, and you'll find your path to your own deepest peace and happiness.

I have never regretted that decision I made as a senior at Marquette High in Milwaukee.

# Three

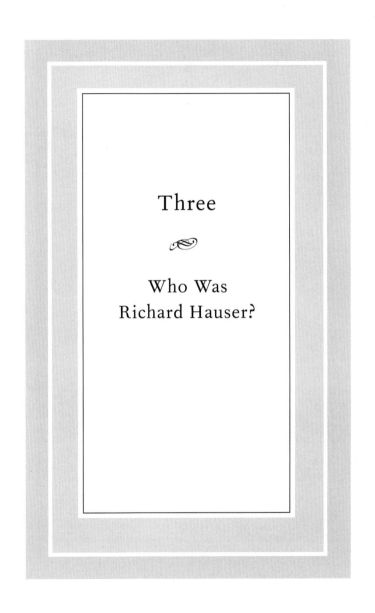

## Who Was
## Richard Hauser?

## RICHARD J. HAUSER, SJ
June 22, 1937–April 3, 2018

Born and raised in Milwaukee, Wisconsin, Fr. Hauser was the oldest of six children. He entered the Wisconsin Province of the Society of Jesus in 1955 and was ordained a priest in June of 1968. Fr. Hauser had a bachelor of arts in philosophy and a master's degree in American history from St. Louis University, and a doctorate in religion and religious education from The Catholic University of America.

Fr. Hauser had a long career at Creighton University in Omaha, Nebraska, as a professor in the Department of Theology. From his earliest days on campus in 1972, Fr. Hauser proved to be a source of spiritual inspiration to Creighton students. His inauguration of the candlelight Mass and his taking on of the directorship of Creighton's programs in theology, ministry, and Christian spirituality were in keeping with what he always felt his fundamental calling was: to help all people recognize God's presence in their lives.

He was the author of three books: *In His Spirit: A Guide to Today's Spirituality* and *Moving in the Spirit: Becoming a Contemplative in Action* (both available from Wellspring), and *Finding God in Troubled Times*. In his writings, Fr. Hauser examined the topics that Catholics are concerned about on a daily basis, including spirituality in our world today, the unique role of the Holy Spirit, and understanding suffering in the human experience.